little hands
SAND

Rachel Matthews

Chrysalis Children's Books

You can find sand in deserts and on beaches.
Sand is made up of tiny pieces of rock.

Sand provides a home for many creatures.

Run your fingers over some soft, dry sand.

What does it feel like?

Scoop up a handful of sand. What happens?

5

Walk through a pile of dry sand.
What happens? What does it feel like?

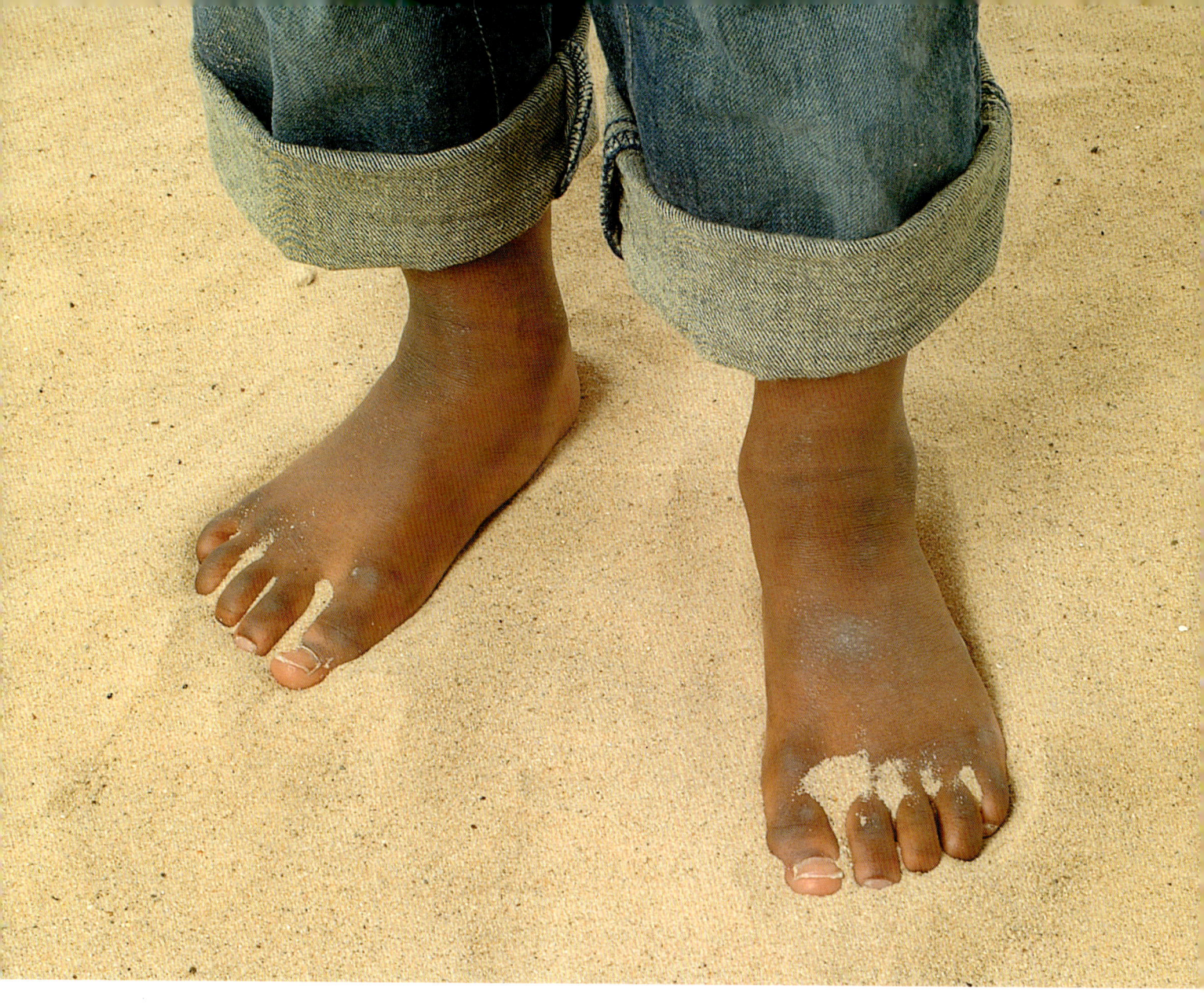

How does the sand feel between your toes?
Does it stick to your skin?

Shake some sand in a pot with a lid.
What sound does the
sand make?

Fill an empty pot
with sand.

How many
spoonfuls
can it hold?

Collect containers of
different shapes
and sizes.

Pour sand into
each container.

Turn one pot upside down.
What happens to the sand?

How is sand different
when it's wet?

Run your fingers
across some wet sand.
What does it feel like?

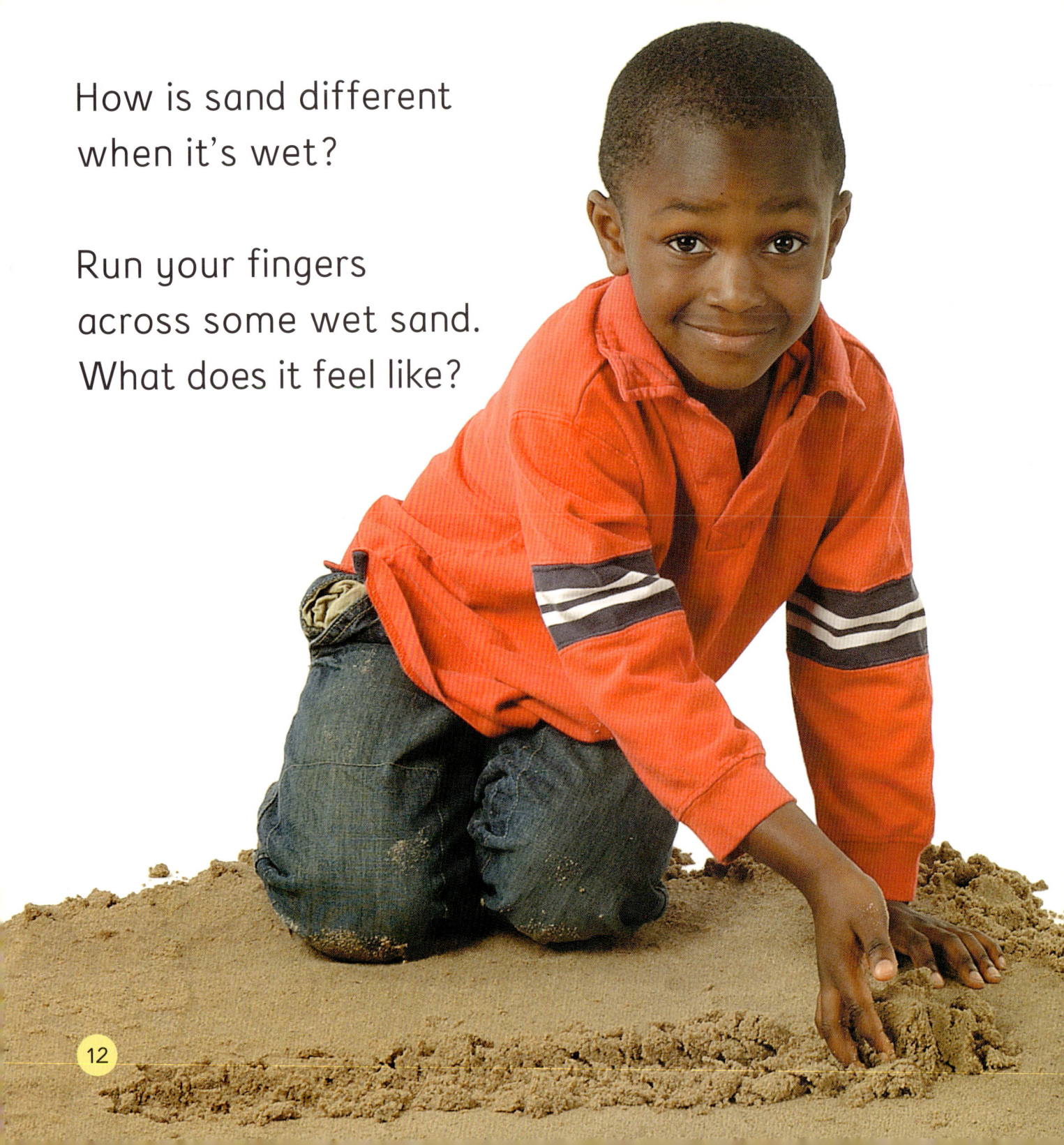

Try drawing in the
sand, or writing
your name.

Walk across some wet sand.
What does it feel like? Can you see your footprints?

Scoop up a handful of wet sand.
What do you notice?

Fill containers of different shapes and sizes with wet sand.

Turn one upside down.
What happens?

17

Try decorating the sand
shapes you've made.

What happens if something heavy lands on top?

People can build with sand.
Look at these amazing sand sculptures.

These sacks are full of sand. People use sand bags to stop water flooding into towns and villages.

Start a treasure hunt! Hide some things in a tray of sand.

Who can find them and guess what they are?

Notes for teachers and parents

Pages 2–3
Discussion: Encourage the children to discuss their own experiences of sand. They may have noticed some properties of sand while playing in a sandpit, or making sandcastles on the beach. The discovery that sand finds its way into every crease of clothing can illustrate that it is made up of tiny pieces of rock.
Activity: The children could try to separate a single grain from a small pile of sand.
Discussion: Showing photographs can help the children to discover how sand provides a habitat for a variety of creatures.

Pages 4–7
When setting up equipment for sand play, position the trays at different heights to suit the range of children.
Discussion: Compile a list of rules for sand play, eg. wearing protective clothing, taking turns, not throwing sand. Talk about why each rule is important.
Activity: When you judge the children are ready, you could introduce the idea and the vocabulary of solids and liquids and point out how sand is unusual: the grains of sand behave as a liquid, filling any shape of container they are poured into, just as water does. Provide a range of equipment such as sieves, funnels and containers of different sizes and shapes, so that the children can predict and then test how sand will behave.

Pages 8–11
Activity: The children could make and decorate their own percussion instruments filled with differing amounts of sand.
Activity: Sand play is an ideal way to introduce the concept of capacity. The children could fill a spade or cup with sand and count how many of them it takes to fill up a given container, then compare results.
Discussion: Show the children a sand timer and encourage them to describe how it works. Discuss how they could use it at home or at school, eg. to time a boiling egg or to make sure everyone has an equal turn during a game or period of play.

Pages 12–15
Activity: Make handprints and footprints in wet sand.
The children could practise writing individual letters, noticing the hand movements required to form each one. You could show them pictures of Japanese Zen sand gardens. The children could use rakes and other tools to make their own patterns in a tray of sand.
Activity: The children could explore ways of moving across or through a large tray of sand. Encourage them to use a range of vocabulary to describe their movements, eg. tread, tiptoe, creep.
Discussion: Ask the children to predict how easy or difficult it would be to lift, walk on or run through both wet and dry sand.

Page 16–19
Activity: Experiment with different-shaped moulds to make sand sculptures. Show the children pictures of sand-sculpture competitions and discuss the differences between these and sculptures made from different materials.
Activity: The children could predict (and then test) which of a collection of objects will be too heavy to be supported by a sandcastle they have made. They could place a container on top of the sandcastle and predict how many marbles they will be able to add to it before the sandcastle begins to collapse.

Page 20–21
Activity: Make sand pictures by sprinkling different colours of sand onto glue-covered card, or by mixing sand into paint.
Activity: Use different grades of sandpaper on a range of surfaces, eg. plastic and wood, to show the abrasive effect.
Discussion: You could discuss with the children how sand is used, eg. in building, flood protection and in the manufacture of glass.

Page 22
Activity: The children might like to build an obstacle course in a sand tray, around which they could navigate a toy car, using directional and positional language, eg. around, along, through.

Index

First published in the UK in 2005 by
Chrysalis Children's Books
An imprint of Chrysalis Books Group Plc
The Chrysalis Building, Bramley Road
London W10 6SP

GW282917-0

Copyright © Chrysalis Books Group Plc 2005

ISBN 1 84458 177 2

British Library Cataloguing in Publication Data for this book is available from the British Library.

Associate publisher Joyce Bentley
Project manager and editor Penny Worm
Art director Sarah Goodwin
Designer Patricia Hopkins
Picture researchers Veneta Bullen, Miguel Lamas
Photographer Ray Moller

The author and publishers would like to thank the following people for their contributions to this book: Ruth Thomson, Blaise Riley Snow and Mollie Worms.

Printed in China

10 9 8 7 6 5 4 3 2 1

Typography Natascha Frensch

Read Regular, READ SMALLCAPS and Read Space; European Community Design Registration 2003 and Copyright © Natascha Frensch 2001-2004
Read Medium, Read Black and Read Slanted Copyright © Natascha Frensch 2003-2004

READ™ is a revolutionary new typeface that will enhance children's understanding through clear, easily recognisable character shapes. With its evenly spaced and carefully designed characters, READ™ will help children at all stages to improve their literacy skills, and is ideal for young readers, reluctant readers and especially children with dyslexia.

Picture acknowledgements
All reasonable efforts have been made to ensure the reproduction of content has been done with the consent of copyright owner. If you are aware of any unintentional omissions please contact the publishers directly so that any necessary corrections may be made for future editions.
Alamy Images: Photomadnz FC (TR), 20, Ecoscene: Alan Towse 21;
NHPA Limited: Stephen Dalton 3; © DigitalVision: FC (TC), 2.